Tommy Nuñez:
NBA Referee

Taking My Best Shot

Barbara J. Marvis

A Mitchell Lane Multicultural Biography
• Celebrating Diversity •

ABOUT THE AUTHOR

Barbara Marvis has been a professional writer for nearly twenty years. She is the author of several books for young adults, including **Famous People of Asian Ancestry** and **Famous People of Hispanic Heritage**. She holds a B.S. degree in English and Communications from West Chester State University in West Chester, Pennsylvania, and an M.Ed. in remedial reading from the University of Delaware. She and her husband, Bob, currently live with their four children in northeastern Maryland.

Library of Congress Catalog Card Number: 95-80603

Second Printing

Your Path To Quality Educational Material

P.O. Box 200
Childs, Maryland 21916-0200

Table Of Contents

ACKNOWLEDGMENTS

The author wishes to acknowledge with gratitude the generous cooperation of Tommy Nuñez; Mary Ann Nuñez; Kino Flores; Father Blaise Cronin; Johnny Nuñez; Ray Aguilar; Ted Podleski; José Ronstadt; Donnie Nuñez; Colleen Whitman; and Tommy Nuñez, Jr. Gracious appreciation also goes to Elaine DagenBela, National Coordinator of the Hispanic Heritage Awards.

PHOTOGRAPH CREDITS

pp. 6, 13, 14, 19 courtesy Tommy Nuñez; p. 21 courtesy Brad Morris; pp. 22, 24 courtesy Father Blaise Cronin; pp. 26, 29, 30, 33, 35, 36, 42 courtesy Tommy Nuñez; p. 44 Rick Stewart/Allsport and Referee Magazine; pp. 46, 47, 48, 49, 50, 53, 58, 64, 69 courtesy Tommy Nuñez; p. 72 courtesy Father Blaise Cronin; pp. 74, 76 (middle) courtesy Tommy Nuñez; p. 76 (top) courtesy Tommy Nuñez, Jr.; p. 76 (bottom) courtesy Colleen Whitman; p. 78 courtesy Tommy Nuñez.

INTRODUCTION
By José Ronstadt

The world of Tommy Nuñez is a constant reminder of the inner strength everyone must have to achieve. His roots are deep in the barrios of Phoenix, Arizona, and in the souls of many of us. He labors in a professional world that two decades ago young Mexican Americans could not have imagined existed, much less a seventeen-year-old expelled from school for being "incorrigible." I have known Tommy Nuñez as a friend and I have followed him as the first and only Mexican American in the National Basketball Association (NBA). One would think that twenty-three years of being "the one and only" would have drastically changed him. Success sometimes makes people forget their past; but not Tommy Nuñez. He is a product of the barrios: tough neighborhoods – Ninth Street and Washington, Dupa Villa Projects – that coexist in such cities as San Antonio, Chicago, or Los Angeles; neighborhoods where survival becomes the central character in the lives of all its residents. He has never forgotten the poverty of his childhood. He knows the total significance of El Barrio: heart and pride, courage and determination, persistence and respect. This barrio attitude nurtures his indomitable spirit to give hope to the lives of others. It motivates him to fight against the stereotypical poor image that many have of Latino neighborhoods throughout the country. This is what clearly defines his commitment to youngsters who excel in hope but lack in opportunities. As an adolescent Tommy Nuñez did not appreciate the value of education, but now he preaches that education is the most secure road to success: "Make Your Move . . . Academics thru Athletics!"

Every year Tommy Nuñez travels over two hundred thousand miles and referees more than eighty games. Thousands of people see him throughout the year in every major city in this country. Every year, between stops, he visits the local youth centers, referees fund-raising all-star games, and speaks at elementary and secondary schools. He knows that the world of professional basketball is not open to most, but to a few, and not necessarily to the most gifted. He knows the playgrounds in the inner cities are factories of futile dreams. Perhaps that is why he constantly challenges all of us to be inclusive, to be respectful of the hopes and aspirations of others. Young academic warriors dominate Tommy's Dream Team, coached by people like himself, who "can talk the talk . . . and walk the walk."

José Ronstadt is host of *Hola, Los Angeles* for KVEA-TV in Los Angeles, California.

At sixteen, Tommy Nuñez rarely attended school anymore. Although he was enrolled at Phoenix Union High School for his junior year, it was unusual for him to show up for class. By late 1955 most school officials just assumed that Tommy had dropped out.

Tommy was running around with very little direction in his life. He answered to no one. From the time his mother and father divorced when he was eleven, Tommy lived with his grandmother, his aunt, his friend Ray's family, and at times he was even on the street. "By the time I was fourteen or fifteen," Tommy says, "I had run out of things to do. The only thing left to do was to get into trouble. The housing projects might be fun when you're little, but they're not much fun when you get older." It was not very long before Tommy was in trouble with the law.

> "By the time I was fourteen or fifteen, I had run out of things to do. The only thing left to do was to get into trouble."

Tommy knew how to drive a car long before he was old enough to drive one. In Arizona the legal driving age is sixteen – with a parent's permission. But Tommy was driving when he was just fifteen – without a license, of course. His friend Ray Aguilar remembers what the two of them used to do: "Tommy and I would push his brother Joey's car out of the projects at night. Then we'd either jump-start it down the road, or we'd hot-wire it. Sometimes we just stole the keys. We'd go riding around all night long." Tommy remembers that they always tried to put the car back exactly where they had found it so Joey wouldn't know they had touched it. Tommy got caught driving without a license many times, and he received several warnings from the police. When he was about sixteen and a half, his mother agreed to sign for him to get a license. Finally, Tommy could drive legally. But his troubles were just beginning.

One hot day in August of 1955, when he should have been in school, Tommy borrowed his Uncle Joe Fierros's car and went out cruising. He was not looking very carefully when he turned a corner not far from his aunt and uncle's home. He sideswiped a parked car. At first he thought he might stop – it was the right thing to do. Then he noticed there was someone sitting in the car. And then he remembered all the other traffic violations he had recently received. Instead of stopping, he kept going.

The woman sitting in the car carefully copied the license number from the back of the car that hit hers. She immediately called the police.

> Tommy knew how to drive a car long before he was old enough to drive one.

By the time Tommy returned to Uncle Joe and Aunt Helen's house, the police were waiting for him. It was his fourth traffic violation that month.

Tommy was taken to the police station – again. The officers were tired of giving Tommy warnings. One of the officers said, "I'm about ready to let you take your chances in front of the judge. Maybe he'll fine you, or even put you in jail! But I'll give you one more chance to stay out of trouble. You can join the Marines – or else!"

Tommy's Family Tree

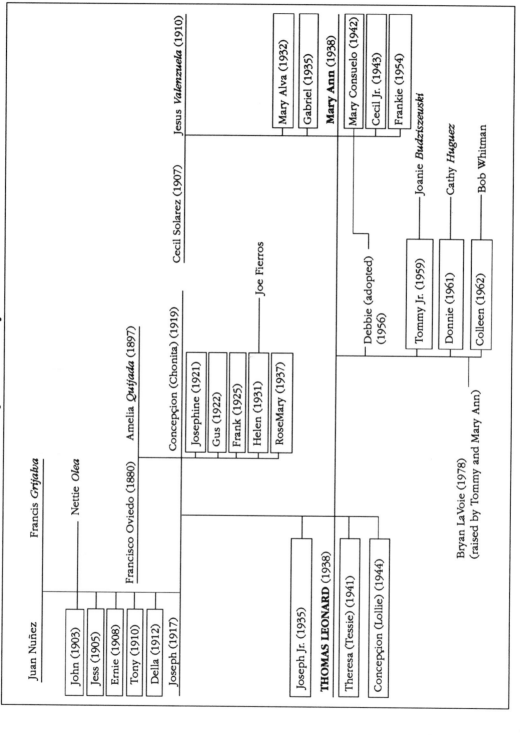

In Benson, Arizona, Tommy's grandparents, Francis (Grijalva) and Juan Nuñez, owned a ranch they called *Tres Alamos*. [*Alamo* is a type of poplar tree that grows in the desert; *tres* means three.] They raised cattle and horses for many years. They had six children. Their first son, John, was born in 1903; then Jess, Ernie, Tony, and Della were born. The youngest child, Joseph (Tommy's father), was born in 1917, nearly fourteen years after John.

> The youngest child, Joseph (Tommy's father), was born in 1917, nearly fourteen years after his oldest brother, John.

The economy brought hard times to Francis and Juan in the early 1900s, and they lost the ranch. Juan went looking for work. He relocated the family to Santa Maria, California, where he found work breaking horses for wealthy ranch owners. The family remained in Santa Maria for many years.

When John married Nettie Olea sometime in the 1920s, his mother and his brother, Joseph went to live with them in Phoenix, Arizona. They stayed for several years. John and Nettie had a son, Johnny, born in 1928. Their daughter Rose was born in 1933. John's brother Joseph was only eleven years older than his son, Johnny, and for a while, little Johnny felt that Uncle Joseph was more like an older brother than an uncle.

As a young boy, Tommy's father was always in trouble. John had to bail him out many times in his life. Joseph was a loner and never much of a social person. He didn't care much about school, either. In 1933, when he was only sixteen, he married Chonita (Toni) Oviedo, who was only fourteen at the time.

As a young boy, Tommy's father was always in trouble.

Toni was born and raised in Phoenix, Arizona. Toni's father, Francisco, was born in Spain, and her mother, Amelia (Quijada), was born in Mexico. Francisco and Amelia Oviedo had six children. Their first child, Chonita, whose given name was Concepçion, was born in 1919. Then Josephine, Gus, Frank, Helen, and RoseMary were born. Chonita, in contrast to her husband, Joseph, was a very social and outgoing person. She always had lots of friends.

Joseph moved his young bride to Santa Maria, California, where he had spent much of his early childhood. In 1935 their first child, Joseph Jr., was born. Their second son, Thomas Leonard Nuñez, was born on September 10, 1938. Theresa (Tessie) was born three years later in 1941, and Concepçion (Lollie) was born in 1944. (Tommy also has two half brothers, Steve and Timmy Nealis from his mother's second marriage to Seymour [Steve] Nealis.)

In Santa Maria, Tommy's father worked for the Coca-Cola Bottling Company and in construction cleaning windows. But Toni had asthma and the climate was difficult for her in California. The family returned to the Phoenix area in 1944. Tommy was only five.

Tommy's father, Joseph

Tommy's mother, Toni

Tommy, center, at about eleven years old, with friends
Moises Moya on left and Alfred Arvizu on right

SCHOOL YEARS – ACTING UP AND ACTING OUT

When Tommy was a youngster, his parents worked very hard. Without an education, they both labored long hours for very little pay. It was never enough to support the family. Both sets of grandparents lived nearby and the extended family was very close. His grandparents would watch him and his siblings while his parents worked. Although his family had very little money, he had lots of cousins and friends to play with. They made their own fun. Tommy grew up poor, but he never really knew the difference until he was in his teens.

Tommy was enrolled for first grade at Garfield Elementary School in 1944. His first few years were uneventful. But Tommy never took school seriously and eventually started getting in trouble. He enjoyed talking back to the teachers. He was a smart aleck and often disrupted class. His parents never stressed to him the importance of education.

> Tommy grew up poor, but he never really knew the difference until he was in his teens.

Because he and his parents moved so much, Tommy attended three different primary schools. He attended Garfield Elementary School until 1947. He attended Monroe Elementary School for fourth and fifth grades, and he spent sixth, seventh, and eighth grades, until 1952, at Edison Elementary School.

Tommy hung around with other kids in his neighborhood who also weren't interested in school. By the time he was in sixth grade, his family had moved to the Dupa Villa Housing Project in East Phoenix, which was a very poor part of town.

Tommy was constantly fighting with the other kids at school, and he was often suspended for his behavior. "We used to criticize everybody's mama," says Tommy, "long before it was fashionable. I'd yell, 'Your mama wears combat boots' to someone loud enough and long enough for him to go ballistic on me. Next thing I knew, someone would be punching me and of course I would have to defend myself. I'd fight all day long. The teachers would get sick of this and send me to the principal. My mother would have to come bring me home. But she never said anything to me about my behavior. If she had even grounded me just once for getting in trouble, it might have sunk in, but she never did."

Despite the facts that he had no respect for authority, he was arrogant, and he had a smart mouth, Tommy was not stupid. "I made B's and C's," says Tommy, "without ever trying. I never did any homework – I think out of defiance – and I paid no attention in school. But I never

> **Tommy was constantly fighting with the other kids at school, and he was often suspended for his behavior.**

failed anything. Can you imagine what I could have done had I been interested in school and done my work?"

His teachers were always trying to make Tommy be responsible. But he never really understood what that meant. His parents were never around, so he had very little guidance at home. Tommy remembers one special teacher at Edison Elementary School, Mr. Tanno, who was always there for him. He tried hard to keep Tommy out of trouble. He told him about self-respect and respect for others, but Tommy was still too young to understand. It was years later before Mr. Tanno's message would hit home.

Things only got worse for Tommy as he grew older. His parents' marriage had never been good. They were always fighting, and eventually the marriage broke up. His parents divorced when Tommy was eleven and in sixth grade. His father moved back to Santa Maria, California, and Tommy saw him only occasionally, usually in the summer. His father never took much responsibility for any of the children after the divorce.

It was difficult enough to make ends meet when Tommy's mother and father were both working to support the family. After the divorce, it was nearly impossible. Tommy says he knew he was poor, but, like everyone else in his neighborhood, he was just having fun, going nowhere. "I knew I wasn't living in the best of conditions," recalls Tommy. "I had very low self-esteem. I certainly didn't look as good as the kids with money. It took a while for me to realize that the other kids could buy new clothes for a school

Tommy remembers one special teacher at Edison Elementary School, Mr. Tanno, who was always there for him. He tried hard to keep Tommy out of trouble.

"It took a while for me to realize that the other kids could buy new clothes for a school dance, but I had to wear whatever my brother Joey had outgrown."

dance, but I had to wear whatever my brother Joey had outgrown."

Tommy's mother remarried several years later, but Tommy never really felt a part of her life after that. Eventually, his mother married several more times, and this instability contributed to the confusion that was part of Tommy's everyday life. Tommy sometimes jokes that he was just another "resident" in her house. His mother was always working and she was never around. So Tommy went to live with his grandparents. His grandmother (Francis) Nuñez was always good to him, and he could hang out there anytime he wanted. He loved the way she could make Cream of Wheat cereal with no lumps! Big Nana and Tata Oviedo also lived nearby, and Tommy stayed with them often. His sister Tessie went off to live with Aunt Helen (their mother's sister). The children were always with family, but they were no longer all together under one roof.

Since his family was very poor, if Tommy wanted any spending money, he had to earn it himself. His first job was shining shoes at Mike's Barbershop. Everyone in the neighborhood hung out at Mike Baca's all-Mexican barbershop. Each week, Tommy would clean the shop for a ten dollar bonus. And every Saturday, Mike let Tommy drink one beer. With Tommy's father living in California, Mike became just like a father to Tommy.

One hot summer day when he was eleven or twelve, Tommy remembers that he went on a field trip with the Boys Club to Prescott, Arizona. Prescott is about ninety miles from Phoenix, and they rode there on a big bus for the weekend. Phoenix, Arizona, has a large minority population, but just outside the city, the ethnic makeup

of the population shifts dramatically. Tommy was not prepared for this change. About thirty boys arrived at Granite Dell to go swimming. All the Anglo boys got to go swimming and the rest of the boys had to stand outside the fence and watch. Tommy and some of his friends did not understand at the time why they weren't allowed to swim. It was years later before he understood

Tommy (in center of picture, sitting down) with the Boys Club

> The Boys Club occupied a lot of Tommy's time when he was growing up. He was kicked out for life, however, when he was only thirteen.

that most public places did not allow nonwhites to go swimming at that time.

The Boys Club occupied a lot of Tommy's time when he was growing up. He was kicked out for life, however, when he was only thirteen.

"Seven of us went to the rodeo for the Boys Club to clean up after the rodeo was over," says Tommy. "The Boys Club would get a donation and we'd get a few bucks for our effort. Well, the soda machines still had syrup in them and the popcorn machine still had crumbs, and pretty soon we all started drinking the syrup and eating popcorn crumbs. The next thing I knew, we started throwing the crumbs at each other and slopping the syrup all over the machines. We ended up doing a lot of damage to the place. We made it a bigger mess than what we were being paid to clean up! But that wasn't the end. My friends elected me to be the spokesman and said I should go ask for our five dollars' pay, despite all the destruction we caused. Well, that was the last straw. The guy went ballistic on me and told me I was out of the Boys Club – forever!"

In school, Tommy's only interest was sports; it was his only motivation to stay in school. He played baseball, basketball, and football. St. Mary's High School, a private Catholic school in Phoenix, not only had a great academic reputation, but it also had a wonderful athletic program. Tommy would have given anything to be able to play sports for St. Mary's. His cousin Johnny Nuñez had been an honor student and graduated from St. Mary's. Several other cousins were at St. Mary's doing very well. But the tuition

at St. Mary's was well out of reach for Tommy's family. It did not seem possible that he could attend. Then one day Tommy was given the opportunity to attend this prestigious private school. St. Mary's gave him a full scholarship (St. Mary's provides financial aid for many of its students), and Tommy could not believe his luck. Attending St. Mary's meant the world to him.

Tommy's baseball team won the state league championship in the summer of 1951. Tommy's coach, Brad Morris (on right) saved this picture. Tommy is in the back row, second in from the left.

Part of the inside campus of St. Mary's High School with a view of the original entrance to the old school

In 1952 St. Mary's High School had about six hundred students. It had a good racial mix for a private inner-city Catholic school, though at the time most of the students were Anglos. About 10 to 20 percent of the students were minorities, about 50 percent of the students received some financial assistance to attend St. Mary's, and 90 percent of the students graduated and went on to pursue a higher degree. But Father Blaise Cronin, who has taught at St. Mary's since 1944, remembers that there was no coeducation at that time. "The girls went to class in one building and were taught by the nuns," he remembers. "The boys went to school in another building about two blocks away and were taught by the Franciscan Fathers. There were about twelve priests who taught the boys, and three or four coaches. They shared a cafeteria with the grammar school and they had dances together, but the education was separate."

Father Blaise Cronin remembers that there was no coeducation at that time. "The girls went to class in one building . . . The boys went to school in another . . ."

Father Blaise continues, "Tommy was taught in an all-boys environment and boys tend to be a little rugged. Tommy was the little happy-go-lucky kid who just wouldn't settle down. I call kids like Tommy 'the original sin in motion.' Tommy was just never doing the things he was supposed to be doing."

This is how St. Mary's looked when Tommy attended in the 1950s.

"I knew I was very lucky to get the chance to go to St. Mary's," says Tommy, "but I still did not straighten up. I was just an inner-city kid trying to survive. No one put any priority on my education. We did not speak about school at home. We didn't talk about homework or world events or civic responsibility. My parents were not very scholarly or educated, and they were mostly concerned about paying rent and feeding the family. There was nothing in my lifestyle that made me understand there was anything better than what I knew."

At St. Mary's, Tommy was a discipline problem. His teachers complained that he was a class clown and that he did not follow the rules. He talked back, and he was constantly fighting. Father Blaise remembers that Tommy was suspended twice, but he was always allowed to return. Then one day he went too far.

Tommy was to play in a baseball game for St. Mary's one afternoon. He played shortstop. His mother and father had never been able to come see him play. But this day was going to be different. Tommy's father was coming from California to watch the game. This meant an awful lot to Tommy, and he was looking forward to it. But early that afternoon, Tommy got in trouble with Father Bryan. As punishment, Father Bryan told Tommy he could not play in the game. Tommy was crushed. His father was coming a long way to see him play. He just had to play. So he did. He never told his coach that Father Bryan said he couldn't play. Tommy simply ignored Father Bryan's punishment.

At the end of the game, Father Bryan realized that Tommy had disobeyed him. "Why did you play when I told you not to?" he asked. Tommy did not tell him that his father was at that game – the first game he had ever seen Tommy play. He did not feel he owed anyone an explanation. And he didn't want anyone to think he was a wimp! So he did not answer, and he was

> At St. Mary's, Tommy was a discipline problem. His teachers complained that he was a class clown and that he did not follow the rules.

asked to leave St. Mary's – permanently. It was just ten days before the end of his sophomore year. He received no credit for his entire last semester.

The following year, in August 1954, Tommy had to enroll at Phoenix Union High School. By then he had lost all interest in school. He hardly ever showed up for class. He wasn't sure where

Tommy is number 12 on the St. Mary's football team. He is shown fifth from the left, in front.

he was living anymore. Sometimes he was out on the streets all night. His close friend Ray Aguilar remembers the situation: "I was at Tempe High at the time. I first met Tommy after school one day when he was hanging out at Garfield Elementary School, which was right by the projects where his mother lived. There was a girls' softball game going on and Tommy used to like to watch. I had come to see the game, too. Tommy really didn't have anyone to answer to. No one took responsibility for Tommy except Tommy. His mother was always busy working or trying to get her life together. Tommy lived with relatives, but no one family member was raising him. After we became friends, he often stayed at my house. My parents had ten children and we lived in a two-bedroom house, but we always made room for one more. Tommy loved the tortillas that my mother made. My father worked at an elementary school, and sometimes they would have butter left over and they would give it to him. My mom would make tortillas with butter on the grill, and that was a real treat for us. Tommy would eat the tortillas one after another as they came off the grill."

That same year, Tommy met a lovely young lady named Mary Ann Solarez, an honor student at Phoenix Union High School. They were both fifteen years old when they met, and they were also both involved with the Catholic Youth Organization at St. Mark's Church. Tommy spent a lot of time with Mary Ann. Her family accepted him right away, and he felt very comfortable with her parents. He envied the fact that she had a stable two-parent home. Her father came home from work each evening and the family ate dinner together. Tommy could see right away that he would like to be a part of a family like that.

"My mom would make tortillas with butter on the grill, and that was a real treat for us. Tommy would eat the tortillas one after another as they came off the grill," remembers Ray.

Tommy completed the 1954–55 school year at Phoenix Union. Since he was a semester behind, he really only completed the first semester of his junior year. That next summer, Tommy spent three months with his father in Santa Maria.

When he returned to Phoenix at the end of the summer, it was not very long before Tommy was in trouble with the law.

On September 20, 1955, Tommy joined the United States Marines.

One day, Tommy borrowed his Uncle Joe's car and went out cruising. He turned a corner, sideswiped a parked car, and pretended he was going to stop. But then he noticed there was someone sitting in the car. Instead of stopping, he decided to keep on going. The woman in the car got his license number, and the police were waiting for him by the time he returned to Uncle Joe's house. The officer in charge gave him an ultimatum: "You can join the Marines, or else." At that time, the Marines were often used as a place for wayward youth, high-school dropouts, and others who needed to straighten out their lives. So, on September 20, 1955, Tommy joined the United States Marines.

At Phoenix Union High School, Tommy met Mary Ann Solarez.

Tommy was not yet eighteen, so he had to have parental permission to join the Marines. His uncle Gus Oviedo signed for him because his mother wouldn't. She was too angry at him for all the trouble he had been getting into. He talked his friend Kido Valenzuela into joining with him to keep him company. "It'll be lots of fun," Tommy promised as the twosome rode a bus to San Diego for adventure in the Marines. Tommy figured he might end up like John Wayne. . . . Not a chance.

By the time Kido and Tommy got off the bus, a Marine officer was yelling and screaming at them. They started laughing, and the next thing they knew they were doing push-ups all through the night. It did not take long for the Marines to teach Tommy about respect. The punishment for disrespect was so severe, it was no longer any fun for Tommy.

> He talked his friend Kido Valenzuela into joining with him to keep him company. "It'll be lots of fun," Tommy promised . . .

Tommy spent twelve weeks in San Diego and then ended up in infantry training at Camp Pendleton in Oceanside, California. He went to communications school for ten weeks to learn to be a cryptographer, which he enjoyed. He was then assigned to the infantry and he received his first orders to go to Japan. Since Tommy had never been to Japan, he was really looking forward to it. He was stationed in Mt. Fuji, but only got to stay there for five days before he was shipped to Okinawa, which was an independent country at that time, and not a part of Japan. He spent nine months in Okinawa and was then shipped to the Philippines during the problems with Indonesia. He remembers landing on the beach in the Philippines and walking about forty miles across the country to their camp. Tommy enjoyed traveling and visiting new places when he was in the Marines. Yet, with all the places he went, he was never on an airplane. He was part of the sea-going Marines, and they traveled by ship or by bus.

"The Marines really turned my life around," recalls Tommy. "I learned to be responsible for my actions . . ."

The three years Tommy spent in the service taught him more than he had ever learned anywhere else. "The Marines really turned my life around," recalls Tommy. "I learned to be responsible for my actions. I learned about self-esteem and self-respect. I learned how to get along with others and how to control my temper. The drill instructors would not settle for mediocrity. They were very regimented. The Marines made discipline a meaningful word in my life. I was also proud to be a part of the armed services, and this pride allowed me to change the way I

Tommy's platoon in the U.S. Marine Corps

viewed my entire life." The Marines made Tommy grow up.

It was also in the Marines that Tommy earned his GED (Graduate Equivalency Diploma), which enabled him to get his first job. But Tommy says he still didn't know the value of his high school diploma. When he was stationed in Okinawa, someone came around and asked if anyone wanted to earn a GED. Tommy figured he'd go take the test – he had nothing else planned for that day. It was a cinch for him. But, he never even thought about the importance of that degree until he was out of the Marines.

On July 21, 1956, Tommy was home on a three-day pass. He was about to be shipped overseas, and he wanted to get married before he left. He called up his friend Ray and said, "Ray, I decided that Mary Ann and I are going to get married today. I need you to be my best man." Ray says this was totally unexpected. He had no idea that Mary Ann and Tommy were going to get married so soon. Later that morning, Tommy and Mary Ann tried to get married at the courthouse in Phoenix, but the judge would not marry them because Tommy was still under age; at that time in Arizona, you could not get married before you were eighteen unless you were expecting a child.

So Tommy drove his cousin Joe Burruel's car and took Mary Ann to Florence, Arizona to get married. Ray came as Tommy's best man, Mary Rose Fimbres Godinez came as Mary Ann's maid of honor, and Tommy's mother came to tell the judge that Tommy was "really eighteen." They went to the courthouse for a very brief ceremony.

When they returned to Phoenix, Mary Ann's mother said she would not consider Mary Ann and Tommy married unless they had a church ceremony. Father Marcos at St. Mark's Church where Tommy and Mary Ann attended the youth group, had not wanted Tommy to marry Mary Ann. In fact, earlier, he had tried to talk Mary Ann's parents out of allowing the marriage be-

> When they returned to Phoenix, Mary Ann's mother said she would not consider Mary Ann and Tommy married unless they had a church ceremony.

cause he did not think that Tommy would be good for her. Tommy called Father Albert Braun at Sacred Heart Church to ask if they could have a church ceremony there. They went for a Catholic ceremony at five o'clock that afternoon.

Tommy had to be back on duty on Sunday and could not stay with Mary Ann very long. She continued to live with her parents while she finished her last year of high school. She graduated from Phoenix Union High School in June 1957, then worked and managed to save some money while Tommy was finishing his tour of duty.

On September 19, 1958, Tommy got out of the Marines and came home to begin his new life with Mary Ann. The newlyweds rented a house from Mary Ann's aunt. The house was on Thirty-Second Street in Phoenix, around the corner from her parents. At the time, Western Electric was hiring many ex-servicemen, and Tommy was able to get a job with them. They trained him to be a switchboard repairman. Tommy was very lucky to get a good job so quickly, but this job was available to him only because he had earned his GED.

Tommy and Mary Ann returned to Florence, Arizona in 1990 to attend a nephew's wedding. He was married right across the street from the courthouse where Tommy and Mary Ann were married in 1956.

Tommy eventually worked for Western Electric (then part of AT&T) for fifteen years (and nineteen days, but who's counting) in various capacities. Tommy Jr. was born in 1959, Donnie was born in 1961, and Colleen was born in 1962. Tommy and Mary Ann set out to provide a different home life for their children than what Tommy had known – more like the home Mary Ann had known. Tommy and Mary Ann stressed the importance of education to all of their children. They watched out for each of their children and disciplined them well. "If my children ever got out of line," says Tommy, "they were grounded. We let them know we cared about them and we cared how they behaved. We were always there for them. I have to give Mary Ann most of the credit for the good job she did with the kids, because she was around much more than I was. In later years, she was able to stay at home with them, and this made a very positive

> "If my children ever got out of line," says Tommy, "they were grounded."

> "My mom and dad's lives centered around us," remembers Tommy's son, Tommy Jr. "They did everything for us. From the time we entered kindergarten, they always stressed the importance of education."

impact on their lives. We never had any trouble with any of our kids and they all ended up doing very well in school, including Debbie, my niece [see Family Tree on page 10], whom Mary Ann and I adopted when she was thirteen." Tommy worked very hard to keep everyone clothed and fed. Even with his steady work at Western Electric, Mary Ann had to work in those early years to make ends meet.

"My mom and dad's lives centered around us," remembers Tommy's son, Tommy Jr. "They did everything for us. From the time we entered kindergarten, they always stressed the importance of education. They raised us to be self-sufficient. They told us early on that we would need our education to get a good job. As long as we were doing what we were supposed to in school, then Mom and Dad would take care of all the fun things outside of school.

"Dad started a peewee basketball league for us to play in when Donnie and I were small. He raised the money for us to play. He coached my teams right up until high school. Mom and Dad never missed any of my games."

Right out of the Marines, Tommy played some semipro baseball and fast-pitch softball for a few years. He was also interested in the local high school sports. Tommy's cousin Johnny was officiating for the Arizona State Interscholastic Association that governed all high school sports. Johnny began officiating in 1952 to help support his eight children. In 1961 Johnny encouraged Tommy to begin officiating.

Through Johnny, Tommy got involved with the local high school games. He signed up to officiate high school football, basketball, and baseball on the freshman and junior varsity levels so he could make some extra money for his growing family, too. He also officiated at the city leagues, the parks and recreation leagues, and the YMCA. In 1962 Tommy's friend Ray Aguilar joined Tommy, and the two officiated many games together.

"Tommy and I were partners – we officiated a lot of baseball games together," says Ray. "We were in the same association and the same league. We had a lot of fun."

Tommy's involvement with the local games gave him a new perspective on life. He enjoyed officiating, and he was good at it. He liked meeting all the people involved with the local sports and he liked working at something that was as organized as the high school and league sports. It had a great impact on his self-esteem. He enjoyed the respect he was shown as a referee and he liked the people he was associated with. They made him feel good about himself. They made him feel special. He enjoyed the fact that he had some impact on the game. Until then, he felt he had been a nobody; this association made him feel like he was somebody. And it was a great feeling.

Tommy and Ray learned very quickly that officiating was hard work. Not everyone always liked the calls they made, and sometimes the fans would get upset and call them names. "I'd hear a

He enjoyed the respect he was shown as a referee, and he liked the people he was associated with. They made him feel good about himself.

lot of things from the stands," recalls Tommy. But one day things really got out of hand.

Ray and Tommy were working a baseball game together. Ray remembers the game was Camelback High School vs. Alhambra High School. They were both premiere teams in the Valley (Phoenix, Arizona). The winner of this game was to go on to the state championship, and both teams had been undefeated all season. "I think Alhambra beat Camelback," Ray says, "and there were some unhappy fans. Some family members of the third baseman for Camelback were making gestures at Tommy during the game whenever they didn't like a call he made. Tommy didn't answer, but he did make some gestures back. After the game, the boy and his family came out to the parking lot by our truck. Mary Ann and Donnie were also there. The third baseman's father went by me and made this gesture at me, and I just called him a hot dog. Then he went to his car and got a two-by-four and came after me with it. At first Tommy thought this guy was just coming to see me to complain, but when the guy got up to me, he hit me from behind. Pretty soon we were all fighting. It turned into a real brawl. Tommy and I were suspended and put on probation. But we had a good commissioner at the time and this parent had a history of causing problems, so Tommy and I were allowed back."

In 1962 Tommy met Ted Podleski, who, years later, would have a great impact on the direction of his life. (Ted is now the executive director of the Arizona Osteopathic Association.) Ted was coaching an American Legion baseball

> Ray remembers, "The third baseman's father went by me and made this gesture at me, and I just called him a hot dog. Then he went to his car and got a two-by-four and came after me with it."

team then, and Tommy was at one of the games as an umpire. Ted remembers, "I didn't know Tommy at the time, but I had seen him before. I loved his flair and enthusiasm for the game. At this particular game, I was taking a beating. We were losing real bad. He just casually said to me something like, 'You're doing a great job. Keep the faith,' and I thought what a nice thing for an umpire to say. I liked Tommy right away. We visited after the game and became great friends."

Ted and Tommy had sons about the same age. They played youth baseball together and Ted and Tommy coached their teams. The teams traveled all over to play. Ted and Tommy even took them to Mexico every year to compete.

Tommy Jr. remembers how much fun they had during those years. "I remember one day when we went to practice at our park. The field was being irrigated and we couldn't play there. Dad had this late '50s black Chevy Impala. He piled about twelve of us into his car and drove us to another park so we could play.

"After our practice, it was almost like a ritual. Dad would take the whole team to one of the local convenience stores and buy us each a pop. We'd all sit outside on the steps after the game drinking our pop.

"Dad always taught us to be the best we could be. And our team was always the best in the league, too. Everyone wanted to play on Dad's team. It was so much fun. We played baseball on the Creighton League every summer. I think it was the summer I was going into sixth grade. We were in the championship playoffs one Saturday.

"Dad always taught us to be the best we could be. And our team was always the best in the league, too. Everyone wanted to play on Dad's team," Tommy Jr. remembers.

From left to right: *Tommy Jr., Tommy, Colleen, Mary Ann, and Donnie, taken at Colleen's fifteenth birthday coming-of-age celebration,* Quinceañera, *a traditional Mexican custom. There was a mass at Immaculate Heart Catholic Church in Phoenix followed by a reception at Del Webb Townhouse. 800 people attended the joyful celebration in 1977.*

All of a sudden, we were being thrown out of the league. There were two players on our team who lived two houses out of our district. Dad had let them play on our team because they had no other team to play for. They wouldn't have been able to play at all. The officials waited until the day of the championship to disqualify us. We had to forfeit the game and go home. But Dad didn't want any of us to be disappointed. So he went to the store and bought us our own trophy, and then he held a celebration party at our house just the same. Everyone knew we would have won."

Tommy continued to work hard to provide a decent living for his family. In addition to coaching his sons' teams, he continued officiating at the high school level. He got to ref some junior college games, too, but the only four-year college games he ever officiated were for Grand Canyon University.

When the Phoenix Suns became a franchise in 1966, Ted Podleski went to work for them.

Bob Machen, who had officiated high school sports with Tommy for several years, eventually became a ticket manager for the Suns. (Bob Machen is now the director of the America West Arena where the Phoenix Suns play.) One day in 1970, the Suns were playing a summer rookie game against the San Diego Rockets, and Ted and Bob asked Tommy to officiate the game. Tommy thought this might be fun, so he said, "Sure, I'll brush up on the NBA rules."

When Ted and Bob saw Tommy at the rookie game, they were impressed. They asked him if he ever thought of trying out at the National Basketball Association (NBA) referee camp in New York. Ted remembers calling Tommy to see if he would go try out. "Tommy said, 'What! This Mexican?'" Tommy had never even thought about officiating any major league sports. This was way over anything he had ever dreamed about. Ted encouraged him to give it some thought. But Tommy was overwhelmed. "Ted, I don't stand a chance," he told him.

"At the time, I was too afraid I'd fail," recalls Tommy. "I didn't really give it any serious thought. Here I was at thirty years old and I'd never even been on an airplane. I'd never been east of Globe, Arizona, and these guys were talking about going to New York to try out for the big leagues. I said, 'No way!'"

> Ted remembers calling Tommy to see if he would go try out. "Tommy said, 'What! This Mexican?'"

In 1971 Tommy got another chance to ref a summer rookie game for the Suns. Here he met an NBA referee named Darell Garretson (now supervisor of all the NBA referees), who also mentioned to Tommy that he thought he had potential. Ted Podleski, Bob Machen, and Darell put together some letters of recommendation. Darell spoke to Mendy Rudolph, who was chief of staff at the time. Ted spoke to Jerry Coangelo, who was then the general manager of the Phoenix Suns (now a principal owner of the Suns), and with all this support, Tommy was invited to go to Buffalo, New York, to try out for the NBA referee staff. By then he had had some time to think about the opportunity, and he figured he didn't have much to lose just by trying out. After all, he had a steady job, and he really didn't need another one.

. . . with all this support, Tommy was invited to go to Buffalo, New York in 1972 to try out for the NBA referee staff.

Tommy talks to Darell Garretson at his first season game, Phoenix vs. Detroit, on December 13, 1973.

So Tommy traveled to New York. His friends were all sure he'd be right back, but were they surprised when they found out that he was chosen as one of five finalists from many hundreds of applicants! The five finalists went to referee camp with the other permanent referees that summer of 1972. Tommy got the opportunity to officiate five preseason games. He remembers that first preseason game as if it were yesterday.

The game was Chicago at Portland in October 1972, and Tommy was working with Jake O'Donnell. "I was horrendous," Tommy remembers. "I hardly blew my whistle at all, maybe only four or five times in the first half. I was probably wrong every time. I couldn't get the jump ball up high enough. The centers trapped the ball going up on the first toss. I don't think the second one ever came down. I had never worked with guys that tall in my life! Everything I'd learned, everything I'd worked for, I just forgot. It was a very traumatic experience."

But Jake was good to him. He told Tommy that everyone was scared his first time out. "The pros are fifty times the caliber of your best college team," Jake told him. "It's not easy to referee. Just calm down and relax. You'll catch on. Everyone is nervous in his first game."

By the fifth preseason game, Tommy's refereeing had improved, but he was still not confident that he had what it took to be a professional NBA referee. Others were, however.

In 1973 Tommy was offered his first contract with the NBA. He was unsure about whether he should accept it. "I had a secure job with Western Electric at the time," recalls Tommy, "and

I didn't know if I should risk that for the insecurity of a new job. Maybe they would throw me out after one season!"

Sometimes Tommy's calls are not popular.

He called his cousin Johnny to ask his advice. Johnny said, "Quit your job with Western Electric, Tommy. I know you'll make it with the NBA." And Johnny was right.

John Nucatola hired Tommy and was his first supervisor. Mendy Rudolph also supported Tommy. John and Mendy were sure he could make it in the big leagues. They encouraged him to continue and taught him a lot about officiating basketball.

"To be a successful referee," says Tommy, "you can't worry about being popular. You do

The official portrait of the NBA referees, 1995

need to have a reputation for being fair. The official's primary function is to call things that give a player an unfair advantage. We're like highway patrolmen. We don't catch all the speeders, but we get enough to keep the game under control. Pro basketball is the hardest of all the sports to officiate. Things happen very fast."

One thing that doesn't change from high school to professional sports is the fans. They are not always happy with the way a game is going. Tommy still has to concentrate hard in order not to hear what the crowd shouts from the stands. "I only hear what I want to hear," says Tommy, "but some of the best lines I remember are: 'If you want to call something, why don't you call a cab and get out of here?' and 'If you go on *What's My Line?*, they'll never guess what you do for a living!'" Tommy hears a lot of racial slurs along with some funny comments. He says he used to try to remember some of the funniest remarks to use on the refs back at his sons' games.

Tommy with Charles Barkley of the Phoenix Suns

Tommy travels every week wherever he is asked to go. He visits all the NBA cities several times each year. He has taken Mary Ann with him on many of his trips. He never knows exactly where he'll be next. And there are no excused absences. Tommy remembers working when he had the flu. "The only reason you could be absent," he says, "is if your mortician calls." Each referee must work very hard at every game. In between games, they have to work out to keep in shape.

"We're not allowed to associate with the players during the game, either," says Tommy. "We can't travel on the same plane or eat in the same restaurant at the same time. We must be totally impartial. There are NBA observers at nearly every game who watch every move you make. The whole game is filmed and sent back to New York, where each ref is evaluated every season. And keep in mind that wherever we go, we're always the visitors. We have no home court."

A TIME FOR GIVING BACK

Chapter Eight

As time went on, Tommy became very comfortable on the court. As he got more experience, he became a good referee. His job allowed him to give his family things that he never enjoyed growing up. This made him proud. One day he decided he should give something back.

"I didn't dream this career," says Tommy. "I didn't plan it. I didn't even work toward it. I was just lucky and it found me. But since I have had such good fortune in my life, I really wanted to give something back to the community I came from." So, beginning in 1978, Tommy Nuñez began community work in his off-season. All of his work has been for the kids.

Tommy believes that kids get in trouble because they run out of things to do. When children come from poor families, there is no money for entertainment. If their parents are not around much, some kids make their own fun by getting

> "I didn't dream this career," says Tommy. "I didn't plan it. . . . But since I have had such good fortune in my life, I really wanted to give something back."

in trouble. So, as a summer hobby in 1978 and 1979, Tommy worked as a youth counselor for Chicanos Por La Causa, a summer youth training and employment program. This program gave about 130 students between the ages of fourteen and twenty-one lots of fun things to do. Tommy and codirector Ruben Calderon helped the young adults accomplish a great deal in those two summers. They helped refurbish several homes in their neighborhoods and they cleaned garbage and debris from vacant lots. They renovated Cana Hall, owned by Sacred Heart Church, in exchange for rent-free use of the auditorium for recreation, lunches, and rap sessions. The workers were paid the minimum wage and had to qualify on the basis of financial need.

"We told these kids the good things and the bad things," Tommy said. "We wanted them to become productive citizens, and we did it by showing them a little bit of love. We tried to instill self-respect, pride, and responsibility." He was able to share his experiences with these young adults. He told them what he had learned. He thought he had some motivational messages to share, and he was right. The program was a big success. The kids cooperated with one another and hardly anyone was ever absent. The kids liked listening to Tommy because he shared the same background with them. He knew what it was like to grow up disadvantaged. Tommy liked working with these kids so much, he thought he would like to work with children as a career. So he expanded his efforts.

> Tommy was able to share his experiences with these young adults.

In 1980 Tommy was hired by the Arizona Department of Economic Security for their Job Training Partnership Administration Programs, which he does in the summer in the basketball off-season. He has worked at this job every summer to the present. The summer youth employment/training program works with socially and economically disadvantaged youths aged fourteen to twenty-one, who are in school or who have dropped out. The program encourages these young adults to stay in school or, drop back in. It encourages them to learn about the world of work, and gives them a chance to raise their self-image, a chance for some on-the-job-training, and

Tommy is pictured (off to the left) at one of his free Basketball/Stay-in-School Clinics in Sacramento, California, July 1995

a chance to earn some money. Tommy was hired to monitor the program for the state. He visits all the work sites and makes sure everything is in compliance with all laws. He is also a keynote speaker at most of the conferences for the participants.

Tommy has helped at hundreds of community fund-raisers over the years. In towns all over Arizona, Tommy shows up to help the Hispanic community whenever there is a need. José Ronstadt, who currently hosts *Hola, Los Angeles* for KVEA-TV, a Spanish language station in Los Angeles, remembers how he came to know Tommy.

"I used to see Tommy at a lot of the community events," says José. "I was very active in many issues in my community where I grew up in Nogales, Arizona. I was always the master of ceremonies at all of the major community fund-raisers, and year after year Tommy would be there to help in some capacity. Sometimes he'd donate NBA memorabilia for an auction, like autographed NBA things. Tommy has a way of making you feel like you've known him forever, so I can't remember exactly when I got to know him personally.

"One year, when I was general manager for a local television station in Phoenix, the local Big Brothers asked me to help them recruit more Latinos to be Big Brothers. I immediately thought of Tommy. I asked him if he would make a 30-second public service announcement that we could air on TV. We got him all dressed up in his NBA outfit and put him on a basketball court

> In towns all over Arizona, Tommy helps the Hispanic community whenever there is a need.

with a basketball in his hands. The one thing I didn't know about Tommy at the time was that he wasn't fluent in Spanish. [He's much better today now that he's been to Spain many times.] This commercial was for Spanish language TV. All I wanted him to say was: *'Hola, Yo soy Tommy Nuñez.'* But he couldn't get past *'Hola!'* I think Tommy holds the record for the most cuts and bloopers in a 30-second public service announcement. We had to do about one thousand takes!

"One fund-raiser that I vividly remember where Tommy helped me," continues José, "was the time I put together a benefit basketball game for the Red Cross in Nogales, Sonora, in Mexico. [Nogales is a border town. There is a Nogales, Arizona, and, across the border in Mexico, there is a Nogales, Sonora.] The Red Cross in this small town in Mexico was in critical need of funds. I asked some media people that I worked with to get a team together so we could hold a benefit game against some local disk jockeys in Mexico. I took Tommy along to referee the games.

"When we arrived, the gym was packed! And even though we were the ones who brought the referee, all of Tommy's calls were benefiting the Mexican team, which shows that Tommy's no fool. He exchanged pleasantries with the crowd all night. They loved him. Then, when the game ended, a whole bunch of kids rushed up to Tommy to talk to him. All of a sudden, Tommy took off his NBA shirt and handed it to a kid. Next he took off his sneakers and gave them away. Next it was his jacket. These kids were in heaven – and Tommy walked out of the gym in his shorts!"

> "All I wanted him to say was: *'Hola, Yo soy Tommy Nuñez.'* But he couldn't get past *'Hola!'*"

Tommy has also worked for the Arizona Department of Education. In the early 1990s he visited many schools, giving talks to at-risk students. He gave a seminar called "Take Your Best Shot!" In his seminar, Tommy stressed the importance of staying in school, taking care of one's self, and saying yes to life.

Every year Tommy is asked to visit hundreds of schools around the country to speak to the student body. Tommy has learned now that the kids love his NBA clothes, so he often travels well prepared to give away NBA T-shirts and caps. But he doesn't just hand them out indiscriminately. After he is finished his speech, he asks if there are any questions. At first a lot of kids are timid, and not many hands go up. But when Tommy calls on the first person with a question, he throws him or her a T-shirt. All of a sudden, the kids can think of a million questions and hands go up everywhere. Tommy has a way of encouraging active participation!

"These kids listen to professionals – lawyers, doctors, and dentists," says Tommy; "but a lot of [the speakers] don't know what it's like to miss a meal and the kids can't relate to them."

In addition to speaking at schools, Tommy has visited nearly all of the Native American reservations in Arizona and many of the prisons throughout the west. He relates well to all the young people he speaks to. He knows what they have been through and where they might be headed.

> "These kids listen to professionals – lawyers, doctors, and dentists – but a lot of [the speakers] don't know what it's like to miss a meal and the kids can't relate to them."

September 21, 1992
10238 N 46th Ave.
Glendale, Az. 85302

mmy Nunez:

ank you
r sche +
de an
many
way to
you si
in your
yours
that
to di
our
thu
you

much for coming
in, You sense.

Mr. Nunez
I really enj...
you an...

Oc

ur op
se I
will
help
our
e
it
they

?

Dear
Tommy Nunez

Whats up? Well 2 years ago
when I was really messed up
With school I heard you talk
and I thought hard about what
you said and it really made
a difference in my life. I
think that you coming to
Palo Verde and talking to us
is really cool I appreciate
What you are trying to
do for U's young adults
and I respect you very
much and if you could
I would like to meet you
and talk with you. Thank
for helping me with my life.

Sincerely,

Charlie
Shepherd

In 1995, Tommy raised $12,000 from his National Hispanic Basketball Classic Tournament, which he used to award six, two-year college scholarships. Recipients of the award in 1995 were, from left to right: Mike Espinoza, Aixa Rosas, Edra Velasquez, Pete Posada, Jr., and Andy Soto. Juan Rodriguez is missing from photo. Kino Flores, Principal of Carl Hayden High is shown in the background with Tommy.

CARL HAYDEN HIGH SCHOOL
Chapter Nine

One school where Tommy is sure to speak every year is Carl Hayden High School. Carl Hayden High School is part of the Phoenix Union High School District. It is located in the innermost part of Phoenix in an area that was proclaimed one of the most crime-infested areas in all of Arizona. It has one of the lowest per capita incomes in Phoenix, even though the people there work very hard. In most households both parents work, often at two or three jobs each, with very little pay and no benefits. These people make do with what they have. Often the parents work so much, there is no one around for the kids.

The school has about 2,500 students, and about 75 percent of those are Hispanic. Five hundred of the students speak English as a second language, or have limited English capability. Kino Flores has been the principal of Carl Hayden High since 1988.

One school where Tommy is sure to speak every year is Carl Hayden High School.

"Many of our young people work to support families," says Principal Kino Flores, "so we recently became a community high school."

"When I first came here," says Kino, "the school had a mind-set that violence and crime were just part of the community. I didn't buy into that. I implemented some tough disciplinary policies and a dress code. I took out all the lockers and made the kids carry all their books in backpacks so they had no excuse for not making it to class on time. I put extra sets of books in each class for kids who 'forget' theirs at home. I advertised a higher standard and expectation. The kids rose to the occasion. Back in 1990 we had over four hundred disciplinary referrals for the year, and 91 percent were of a violent nature. In 1994 to 1995, we had only one hundred thirteen referrals all year and only 31 percent were of a violent nature."

Carl Hayden has always had a high dropout rate. Until recently, only 39 percent of the students ever finished high school. Principal Flores wanted to give more of the students a chance to earn a diploma. "Many of our young people work to support families," says Kino, "so we recently became a community high school. We offer classes until eight o'clock at night so the students can arrange their class schedules around work. Some of the students even use this flexibility to accelerate their studies and graduate sooner. Everyone here works very hard to make sure these kids have every opportunity to succeed." And it has paid off. Today, 59 percent of the students who enter Carl Hayden High School will graduate.

"Education is so slow to change," remarks Principal Flores. "Years ago, schools sought only to teach reading, writing, and computing. Today our school needs to fill the gaps of all the social problems facing these youngsters. The school is ill-equipped to help in this area. So we try to get various agencies and the business community to help us. One of our community members who has helped these kids immensely is Tommy Nuñez.

"I met Tommy back in 1968, when I was playing ball in high school. Tommy came to ref one of my games. He always did his homework before the games. He knew who the key players were and he would keep them in line. He'd control the game by controlling the key players. He was always talking. I was very impressed with him. I'd run into him about once or twice a season, but then I lost track of him when I went off to college.

"Tommy started helping me when I was the principal at Tolleson. For the past thirteen years, Tommy has been the keynote speaker at all my freshman student body assemblies. Tommy is an inspirational speaker because he speaks from the heart. He speaks the kids' language. He has a unique ability to reach a variety of youngsters: He can speak to the kids in the hood and turn around and talk to the more affluent students just the same.

"Tommy spends a lot of time in the schools developing relationships with the kids. They love him. When he tells the kids he's gonna do something for them, he always follows through. Sometimes he can't remember a kid's name and he'll call me up and say, 'Kino, who was that young

> "Tommy is an inspirational speaker because he speaks from the heart. He speaks the kids' language."

lady I promised. . . ,' and I'll say, 'I don't remember, Tommy.' Then he'll say, 'Find out for me!' Then I'll call him back and tell him who it was. 'Did I promise her tickets to the game? Okay, they're on the way.'

"Kids gravitate to Tommy. He's our personality here at Carl Hayden. He's our celebrity, and many kids are surprised each year when he goes right up to them and talks to them. He's been known to pull money out of his pocket to help some of the kids!

"The biggest compliment I heard about Tommy came from one of our high school teachers. He said, 'Tommy Nuñez will be the only NBA official who will be broke by the time he retires. He gives all his money away trying to help others.'"

Tommy Jr. agrees. "Dad believes in sharing his good fortune with others. He hates to see any children go without what they need. He is always willing to help, though he stresses to them that they have to learn to support themselves. He can help a little bit, but they have to help themselves, too. I remember Dad coming home from a talk at one of the local prisons. He was in his socks. He had given his shoes away to an inmate who admired them but couldn't afford the type of Converse sneakers Dad was wearing. Dad always had another pair of shoes in his closet. But he would have given them away even if they had been the only pair he owned."

"Tommy is so charismatic," continues Kino. "If he were a drinker, which he isn't, he's the type that could sit in one room and drink a beer

"Kids gravitate to Tommy. He's our personality here at Carl Hayden. He's our celebrity."

with the janitor, and then go to another to sip champagne with the Governor. He gets along with any type of individual."

Just what does Tommy tell the young people he speaks to? "I tell them things they want to hear," says Tommy. "Things I would have wanted to hear when I was their age.

"Kids are basically good all over," continues Tommy. "But they are victims of their environment. They don't have role models. It's very difficult for them to be positive when everything around them is negative."

Tommy encourages all young adults to stay in school. "I want them to know what is possible if they complete their education. Education is the number one edge a kid can gain. I share my life story with them so they know I've been there myself. I don't want things to be as hard for them as they were for me."

In 1994 Tommy was honored by the Hispanic Heritage Awards for excellence in sports. The nation's leading Hispanic organizations, which recommend and vote on people for the awards, all gathered at a celebration for Tommy and several other recipients on September 19 at the National Building Museum in Washington, D.C. Since Tommy's work is all about kids, he decided to take one of them to the awards ceremony with him. He called Kino Flores at Carl Hayden High School and said, "Hey, listen, Kino, I've just been notified that I'm receiving the Hispanic Heritage Award. Instead of having an adult personality present this award to me, I'd rather have a young person go with me. Can you find

Tommy encourages all young adults to stay in school. "I want them to know what is possible if they complete their education. Education is the number one edge a kid can gain."

out if there is someone at your high school whom I might have moved or affected? I'd like to take him or her to Washington, D.C. with me." Kino promised he would find someone.

Tommy and Pete Posada at the Hispanic Heritage Awards, along with the U.S. Representative from Arizona, Ed Pastor

"I went on the public address system at school right before lunch," says Kino, "and I announced that Tommy had won this award. I asked if there was anyone out there Tommy had inspired to change and I asked them to come see me in my office.

"After lunch, about 125 youngsters were lined up outside my office! It was phenomenal. I couldn't believe it. I didn't even tell them this might mean a trip to D.C. for them. So what I had to do was to turn this into a contest. I asked them to write me a letter about how Tommy had influenced them or affected their life. About 250 youngsters responded."

Pedro (Pete) Posada, then a Carl Hayden High School senior, won the trip. One of four children born to Mexican immigrants, Pete wrote that he first met Tommy when he was in eighth grade when he came to speak at his elementary school. "At the time, Pete was deeply involved with a gang," recalls Kino. "He said that things Tommy said allowed him to change directions. He wrote about following Tommy's endeavors with the NBA and listening very closely to him when he came to speak at Carl Hayden High."

Pete accompanied Tommy to the awards ceremony and introduced him. It was the first time Pete had ever been on a plane. Tommy said, "I could have taken anyone I wanted with me, maybe one of the NBA players. But that's not what I'm about. I want to help the kids, so it meant more to me that one of them accompanied me to Washington."

Pete also won one of six college scholarships that Tommy awards every year. Pete is the first in his family to attend college. In August 1995, Pete began his college career.

> Pete wrote that he first met Tommy when he was in eighth grade. . . . "At the time, Pete was deeply involved with a gang," recalls Kino.

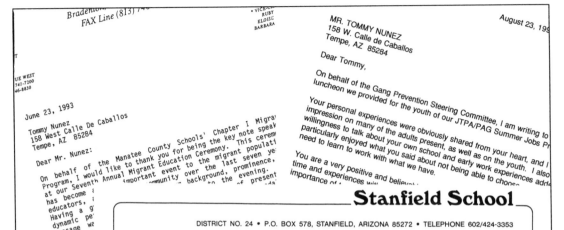

Stanfield School

DISTRICT NO. 24 • P.O. BOX 578, STANFIELD, ARIZONA 85272 • TELEPHONE 602/424-3353

GOVERNING BOARD
YOLANDA GONZALES
JACK KORTSEN, JR.
OLIVIA RODRIGUEZ
JAMES SENSIBAUGH
JOHNNY WHITEHEAD

ADMINISTRATION
DR. BRYANT RIDGWAY, Superintendent
GARY WHELCHEL, Principal

September 8, 1994

TO: Tommy Nunez

FR: Gary Whelchel - Principal

I want to extend my appreciation to you for sharing a few hours with our young people on Wednesday, September 8. You made an impression on our students. They were talking all day about some of the things you said and discussed with them. The hispanic students that you spent some extra time with were extremely impressed. You have become a role model in their lives.

You are to be commended for taking time out of your busy day and schedule to visit Arizona schools. Your work with the youth of this state is making a difference. Thank you very much.

I also want to thank you for the offer of financial support for the coming year. Your generosity in the past has been put to good use assisting our poverty level students. Disneyland is a big treat for our young people, and your help has made it possible for many to attend over the years.

I look forward to our next meeting (Call next year for help with your tournament!!)

Tommy's work for the kids spans many different activities. He has donated his time over the years to referee for such charitable games as Magic Johnson's Summer All-Star Basketball Classic, which benefits the United Negro College Fund, and to give a Youth Basketball Clinic to benefit Chicanos Por La Causa. He puts together free three-day basketball/stay-in-school camps and gets NBA players to volunteer a day of their time to spend with the kids. Some of these basketball camps have been held in Yakima, Washington; West Sacramento, California; and Houston, Texas. In Stanfield, Arizona, Tommy raises money to sponsor many migrant children to go to Disneyland and to buy clothes and food.

But the highlight of Tommy's summer comes every Labor Day weekend when he hosts the Tommy Nuñez National Hispanic Basketball Classic Tournament. The tournament raises funds

. . . the highlight of Tommy's summer comes every Labor Day weekend when he hosts the Tommy Nuñez National Hispanic Basketball Classic Tournament.

for academic and athletic activities for disadvantaged youth. Much of the money goes for college scholarships. Over the years, the event has grown from eight teams participating in 1981 to more than forty teams in 1995. The teams come from around the country. [They even have a league for old-timers: Tommy's friends over forty!] Tommy officiates the games along with many other NBA referees who also donate their time. Every other year, thirty referees come from Spain! All the players are of Hispanic heritage. Tommy says, "Sometimes, all you hear about are the bad things coming out of the barrio. There are so many good things, too. And in this event, I want our people helping our own kids."

Some of the basketball games are played at St. Mary's High School [yes, the same high school Tommy was kicked out of]. North High School, which has two large gymnasiums, and Carl Hayden High School are also sites for the games. Tommy raises funds without charging admission to the games. He gets corporate sponsors such as Coca-Cola; Nestlé; Budweiser; Phoenix Newspapers; Phoenix Greyhound Park; Sportsman's Park of Chicago, Illinois; KTVW Channel 33; and Bank One to donate funds. He raises money from concession sales and team entry fees. In 1995 he raised $12,000 in four days, which was used for two-year community college scholarships for local students.

Tommy's entire family and many of his friends help with the tournament. Mary Ann runs the snack bar. Many people from all ethnic backgrounds come to watch. Sometimes they fill all

> In 1995 Tommy raised $12,000 in four days, which was used for two-year college scholarships.

the stands. There can be anywhere from 300 to 900 people watching any one game. Since the games are free, it keeps a lot of young people entertained over the Labor Day weekend. It is a great time for the entire Hispanic community.

Tommy Jr. holds a golf tournament fund-raiser for the St. Mary's baseball team every year and his father helps out. "Tommy is a horrible golfer," jokes Kino Flores, who also attends Tommy Jr.'s benefit. "He is an embarrassment to the Mexicans. Everyone's goal is not to be paired up with him."

Tommy with son, Tommy Jr. taken at the National Hispanic Basketball Classic, Labor Day weekend, 1995

"We call it 'the St. Mary's experience,'" Tommy Jr. adds. "Dad only plays golf once a year and this is it. You wouldn't believe his golf etiquette. You can hear Dad three holes away!" Even though Tommy can't play golf, he always helps out. A small Catholic high school has no extra funds for many athletic activities; in fact, they have to practice at the city park. The tournament helps raise funds for the kids to continually upgrade their athletic facilities.

Tommy doesn't do any of his work with the kids for the glamour. Many times there is no recognition and he isn't sure how many kids are listening when he speaks. If he helped only one kid turn his life around, Tommy would be happy.

Tommy's son Donnie says, "You can tell how genuine Dad is because his actions are all from his heart. He doesn't do this to impress people. There aren't any reporters around or cameras rolling when he gives kids the shirt off his back or the shoes from his feet."

"The kids who are socially and economically disadvantaged are very dear to me," says Tommy. "They mean a lot to me because of my own background. I want to relate to them. I want to be able to help. I try to instill in them a pride, some dignity. I tell them how to do good things for themselves. I don't tear them down for their poor circumstances. I am always positive. I talk to hard-core kids, many of whom have the same problems I had when I was growing up. They often have no positive role models."

Tommy tells all young adults that they can succeed at anything. They can aspire to any job

> "He doesn't do this to impress people," says Donnie. "There aren't any reporters around or cameras rolling . . ."

they want in life. "Be the best you can be for yourself," he says. "You've got to please yourself. You know right from wrong. You don't have to do drugs. You don't have to belong to gangs. You've got choices. You don't have to be a Rhodes scholar. But you do need a good high school education. You can go on to college, if you want to. It's okay to have any honorable job, but if you want to be the boss, you should strive for that, too. Unless your parents have money or you hit the lottery, you'll have to be prepared to earn your own way. You can't do that without a good education."

Tommy taught these very same lessons to his own children. Each one graduated from St. Mary's High School with honors. Father Blaise, who taught Tommy forty years ago, also taught chemistry to each of Tommy's children. "There is a God in heaven, Tommy!" Father Blaise says. "Your kids are a miracle!"

St. Mary's High School continues today in much the same tradition as it did when Tommy attended. In 1988 the building was moved from downtown Phoenix to make way for the Arizona Center. St. Mary's campus was moved about a mile and a half up Third Street. The ethnic make-up of the school has also changed a little: Approximately 50 percent of the students are Hispanic, 40 percent are Anglos, and about 10 percent are African-American. Many students require financial assistance. But the students still answer a teacher's question with, "Yes, sir," and "Yes, ma'am;" they still wear uniforms; and the St. Mary's Knights keep beating Brophy in football. St. Mary's

"You don't have to do drugs. You don't have to belong to gangs. You've got choices," Tommy tells the kids.

continues to instill in all students that they have an obligation outside their own boundaries – that they are obligated to give back to their community. The Franciscan approach to life is altruistic and idealistic. You can see where Tommy might have learned his values. And though St. Mary's is one of the smallest high schools in Phoenix, its graduates claim some of the best jobs there. St. Mary's graduates fill City Hall, the police department, the fire department, and the legislature.

The new St. Mary's, opened in 1988

Congressional Record

United States
of America

PROCEEDINGS AND DEBATES OF THE *103*[rd] CONGRESS, SECOND SESSION

| Vol. 140 | WASHINGTON, THURSDAY, SEPTEMBER 29, 1994 | No. 139 |

House of Representatives

TOMMY NUNEZ

HON. ED PASTOR
OF ARIZONA
IN THE HOUSE OF REPRESENTATIVES

SEPTEMBER 28, 1994

MR. SPEAKER, I WOULD LIKE TO TAKE THIS OPPORTUNITY TO CONGRATULATE MR. TOMMY NUNEZ WHO WAS RECENTLY HONORED AT THE HISPANIC HERITAGE AWARDS DINNER FOR EXCELLENCE IN SPORTS.

AN ARIZONA NATIVE, MR. NUNEZ GREW UP IN THE DUPA VILLA PROJECTS OF EAST CENTRAL PHOENIX. HE JOINED THE MARINES AND WORKED AS A PHONE-COMPANY SWITCHBOARD REPAIRMAN BEFORE HE BEGAN HIS CAREER AS A REFEREE FOR THE NATIONAL BASKETBALL ASSOCIATION IN 1973. AS ONE OF ONLY 28 MEN WHO ARE OFFICIALS WITH THE NATIONAL BASKETBALL ASSOCIATION, HE IS THE ONLY MEXICAN-AMERICAN TO REFEREE IN THE RANK OF PROFESSIONAL BASKETBALL.

MR. NUNEZ' ACCOMPLISHMENTS ALONE SERVE AS AN INSPIRATION TO MINORITY AND UNDERPRIVILEGED YOUTH. BESIDES SERVING AS A ROLE MODEL, HE IS DEDICATED TO IMPROVING THE LIVES OF OTHERS AROUND HIM.

WHEN HE IS NOT WORKING FOR THE NBA, MR. NUNEZ WORKS FOR THE ARIZONA DEPARTMENT OF ECONOMIC SECURITY JOB TRAINING ADMINISTRATION AS A SUMMER YOUTH EMPLOYMENT MONITOR AND COORDINATES THE TOMMY NUNEZ HISPANIC BASKETBALL CLASSIC. IN ADDITION, MR. NUNEZ TRAVELS TO LOCAL SCHOOLS SPEAKING ON THE IMPORTANCE OF EDUCATION AND TEACHING STUDENTS HOW TO COPE WITH PEER PRESSURE. HE SERVES ON THE GOVERNOR'S COUNCIL ON FITNESS, THE PHOENIX YOUTH COMMISSION AND THE MAYOR'S ADVISORY COMMITTEE FOR SUBSTANCE ABUSE AND COMMUNITY EDUCATION.

MR. SPEAKER, TOMMY NUNEZ IS AN EXCEPTIONAL PERSON WHOM I AM HONORED TO KNOW AND PROUD TO RECOGNIZE. HIS HIGH SENSE OF INTEGRITY AND OUTSTANDING LEADERSHIP HAVE MADE A PROFOUND IMPACT ON THE YOUNG PEOPLE OF ARIZONA. HIS MANY ACHIEVEMENTS AND HIS ACTIVE PARTICIPATION IN THE COMMUNITY MAKE HIM A ROLE MODEL THAT WE CAN ALL ADMIRE AND LEARN FROM. AGAIN, I WOULD LIKE TO TAKE THIS OPPORTUNITY TO CONGRATULATE MR. NUNEZ AND ESPECIALLY TO THANK HIM FOR ALL HE IS DOING TO MAKE A POSITIVE INFLUENCE IN THE LIVES OF THE PEOPLE OF ARIZONA AND THROUGHOUT THE NATION.

Tommy and Mary Ann with their eleven grandchildren: From top to bottom: *Michael, Carissa, Asuzena, Brianna, Jay, David, Kaitlyn, Alex, Bridget, Monique, and Vanessa*

Tommy's children are grown now. Tommy Jr., Donnie, and Colleen were all married in the same year. They all live within five minutes' driving distance. And now, Tommy has eleven grandchildren! His oldest son, Tommy Jr., earned a college degree in business administration from Grand Canyon University. Ironically, he is a teacher at St. Mary's High School. He teaches a personal finance class and a freshman computer class. He is St. Mary's head baseball coach. Tommy Jr. also officiates PAC 10 (Pacific Athletic Conference) college basketball games. He and his wife, Joanie, have twin boys, Alex and Michael, and a daughter, Kaitlyn.

Tommy's second son, Donnie, is a supervisor for the Job Training Partnership Administration in the School and Summer Youth Training and Employment program for Maricopa County. This is the same program that Tommy monitors for the state of Arizona every summer. Donnie

> Tommy's oldest son, Tommy Jr., is a teacher and head baseball coach at St. Mary's High School.

Tommy Jr. with wife, Joanie, daughter Kaitlyn, and twins Alex and Michael

Donnie with wife, Cathy, and daughters Carissa and Brianna

Colleen and husband Bob Whitman with their three children: David, James Joseph, and Bridget

enjoys working with disadvantaged youth for the same reasons his father does. "I know these kids have potential," Donnie says. "I try to help them see how important it is for them to get their high school diploma. I can relate to these kids, too, because I am a lot like my dad. I liked to run around doing mischievous things when I was in high school, just like my dad did. In fact, my dad would kill me if he knew some of the things I did. But I never got caught, and I never crossed over the line. My parents always kept me on the straight path. They were always there for me and I would never dream of embarrassing them." Donnie also referees high school and junior college basketball games. Donnie and his wife, Cathy, have two daughters, Carissa and Brianna.

Colleen and her husband, Bob Whitman, have three children: David, James Joseph, and Bridget. She finished three years at Arizona State and is planning to finish her last year soon. Colleen says she and her dad have argued about everything over the years. When she was little, she could never win an argument with him. She would always end up running upstairs in tears. Now that she is grown, the tables have turned. Tommy runs upstairs – he can't win any arguments with Colleen.

Debbie, a bilingual teacher's aide for the Phoenix Elementary School District, is married to Freddie Santiago. They have three children: Monique, Vanessa, and Shana (Azusena).

Tommy's cousin Johnny Nuñez left the Interscholastic Athletic Association and his job in the fire department in 1963 to return to college, which he had begun many years earlier. After twenty-three years and eight children, Johnny earned his degree from Arizona State University. An article in the local newspaper told of Johnny's accomplishments and he was offered a job with Budweiser. But Johnny turned it down. He had his heart set on becoming a teacher and coach. After seven years' teaching and coaching at Gerard High School, Johnny became a physical education teacher in the Phoenix Union High School District. He taught at nearly every school, including Carl Hayden High, Camelback, Maryvale, East High, and South Mountain High. He retired in 1990 and lives with his wife, Estelle.

Ray Aguilar still lives in Tempe with his wife, Gayle. He is a Unocal gasoline dealer and owns a service station there.

Tommy's father, Joseph, is retired and lives in Santa Maria, California. Of his brothers and sisters, he is the only one alive today. Tommy's mother, Toni, died of cancer in February 1991. Her sister Helen is still alive, but all of her other siblings are deceased.

Both of Mary Ann's parents died recently. Her mother, Jesus, died in November 1993 and her father, Cecil, died in February 1994.

In 1996 Tommy and Mary Ann celebrated their fortieth anniversary. Their commitment to each other has been just as strong as their commitment to their children over the years. They recently bought a beautiful house in Tempe. People asked them why they needed such a big house now that all their children are grown. Tommy says he wants his grandchildren to have

"I can relate to these kids, too," says Donnie, "because I am a lot like my dad."

things he couldn't afford to give his own children. He has a swimming pool, a basketball court, and a swing set so the grandchildren can come over and play every day. And they are still raising kids. Their nephew Bryan LaVoie has lived with Tommy and Mary Ann since he was a baby. Bryan attends St. Mary's High School.

Tommy and friends at Colleen's wedding, May 30, 1987. From left to right, top to bottom: *Kino Flores, José Muñoz, Earl Wilcox, Rudy Santa Cruz, Frank Hidalgo, Henry Peralta, Sal Martinez, Ray Aguilar, Victor Flores, Nick Rios, Tommy, and Ruben Calderon*

Today, Tommy Nuñez is one of only fifty-four people nationwide who earn their living officiating for the NBA. What's more, he is the only Hispanic to officiate for any of the major sports.

Tommy says he'll never forget where he came from. He chooses to remember all the hard times growing up. It's what motivates him to help others. Tommy Nuñez has touched the lives of thousands of young people with his personal story of hardship and success. He stands as a testament to the importance of education, self-respect, and the will to seek the best in life. Tommy knows you can be anything you want to be in America – if you work hard enough.

September 10, 1938	Born Thomas Leonard Nuñez in Santa Maria, California
1944	Family moves to Phoenix, Arizona; Tommy enrolls for first grade at Garfield Elementary
1950	Parents divorce; Joseph returns to Santa Maria
1952-54	Attends St. Mary's High School; plays shortstop on baseball team
June 1954	Asked to leave St. Mary's before end of sophomore year
1954-55	Meets Mary Ann Solarez; attends Phoenix Union High School
September 20, 1955	Joins United States Marines
July 21, 1956	Marries Mary Ann Solarez in Florence, Arizona
1956	Earns GED
September 19, 1958	Gets out of Marines; gets job with Western Electric
1959	Tommy Jr. born
1961	Donnie born; begins officiating high school sports
1962	Colleen born; meets Ted Podleski
1968	Meets Kino Flores and Bob Machen
1970, 1971	Officiates summer rookie game for the Phoenix Suns; meets Darell Garretson
1972	Goes to Buffalo, New York, to try out for the NBA referee staff
October 1972	Referees first NBA preseason game
1973	Offered first contract with the NBA
1978-79	Begins motivational speaking to at-risk youth; youth counselor for Chicanos Por La Causa
1980	Begins job as work site monitor for Arizona Department of Economic Security for JTPA
1981	Begins Tommy Nuñez National Hispanic Basketball Tournament and Scholarship Fund
1990	Gives seminars for Arizona Department of Education
1994	Wins Hispanic Heritage Award for excellence in sports